LONDON'S GEMINI BUSES

DAVID BEDDALL

AMBERLEY

Acknowledgements

My sincere thanks again go to Liam Farrer-Beddall for once again putting his photograph collection at my disposal, and also for taking the time to read through the draft for this book. I would also like to thank Aethan Blake for again providing photographs for this book.

First published 2024

Amberley Publishing
The Hill, Stroud
Gloucestershire, GL5 4EP

www.amberley-books.com

ISBN 978 1 3981 0634 5 (print)
ISBN 978 1 3981 0635 2 (ebook)

British Library Cataloguing in Publication Data.
A catalogue record for this book is available from the British Library.

Origination by Amberley Publishing.
Printed in the UK.

Introduction

The Eclipse Gemini was introduced by Northern Ireland-based Wrightbus of Ballymena. The Gemini was the first double-deck bus body to be built by Wrightbus. Since its introduction in 2001, the model has proved popular with operators in the United Kingdom, the Republic of Ireland and Hong Kong alike. The Eclipse Gemini has a distinctive appearance, with the upper- and lower-deck windows and the destination display being covered by a single, oval-shaped piece of glass.

The Gemini was originally available on the Volvo B7TL chassis, this combination proving popular with both London and other UK operators such as First Group and Lothian. In 2003, the VDL DB250/Gemini combination became available, although in terms of London buses it was only the Arriva operating companies that took stock of this type. The Gemini model available on the DB250 model became known as the Gemini Pulsar. A modified version of the Gemini was introduced in 2006, with slight modifications being made to the appearance, such as the rear of the vehicle becoming more rounded than previous models. In 2008, a new chassis was added to the Gemini range, the hybrid Volvo B5LH. Six of these vehicles were taken into stock by Arriva London. Between 2001 and 2009, 2,555 Gemini-bodied double-decks were supplied to UK operators.

The Wrightbus Eclipse Gemini 2 was introduced in 2008, and was available on the Volvo B9TL and Volvo B5LH chassis. The Gemini 2 again featured the oval-shaped windscreen and top-deck windows. The model again proved popular with bus operators around the country. First Group and Lothian, along with Dublin Bus, again placing orders for the Gemini 2 model. Wrightbus introduced an integral version of the Gemini 2, with components being sourced from VDL, the type becoming known as the VDL DB300. This was again the main type purchased by Arriva London, although a handful of integrals were purchased by other London operators.

A third generation of the Gemini, the Gemini 3, was introduced in 2013, with three demonstration models being placed on loan to London operators in late 2013, before bulk orders were received for 2014 delivery. The original Gemini 3 model was similar in appearance to the Gemini 2, with slight variations in bodywork. However, 2014 saw a change to the front of the Gemini, it being remodelled to look more like the Wrightbus Streetdeck integral bus that had become available. To start with, both this and the original Gemini model were available, but this changed in 2015 when the latter style gave way to the new model. Since its introduction in 2001, over 3,000 Gemini variants have run in service with London operators.

The first pair of Wright Eclipse Geminis arrived in London in July 2001 based on the Volvo B7TL chassis. They were the first of fifty ordered by Arriva London for operation in the Wood Green area. VLW2 (Y102 TGH) is seen about to enter Edmonton Green bus station having completed a journey on the 144 from Wood Green. (Liam Farrer-Beddall)

The first fifty VLW-class Volvo B7TLs with Arriva London were ordered for routes 102, 121 and 141. Further deliveries allowed route 144 to be converted too. VLW9 (LJ51 DFO) is seen at Turnpike Lane, which was a hot spot for the VLW class. It is seen heading towards Edmonton Green. (Liam Farrer-Beddall)

Enfield Town finds a pair of Wright Eclipse Geminis operating the 329 service. Allocated to Palmers Green, VLW16 (LJ51 DGE) is seen closest to the camera, while VLW30 (LJ51 DHK) is seen to the right. (David Beddall)

Another photograph taken in the Turnpike Lane area. The 141 is the longest route to operate from Wood Green, and is the only service to cross the River Thames. VLW59 (LF02 PTX) is seen heading towards London Bridge. A comparison between the original Gemini and the Gemini 2 body style can be made with the pair seen behind. (Liam Farrer-Beddall)

The 221 travels between Turnpike Lane station and Edgware station. VLW77 (LF52 USO) is seen on layover at Edgware station. The original 'cow horn' livery applied to Arriva London buses can be clearly seen in this view. (David Beddall)

Twenty VLW-class Volvo B7TLs were taken into stock at Tottenham in January 2003 for the 139. This was the first of the type for Tottenham. VLW88 transferred to Barking in April 2005, then Stamford Hill in March 2007 before being allocated to Clapton in November 2009. VLW88 (LF52 UPY) is captured by the camera passing through Dalston Junction on route 242 towards Homerton Hospital. (Liam Farrer-Beddall)

Barking received twelve VLW-class B7TLs in March 2003 for route 20. VLW110 (LJ03 MJE) is seen departing Walthamstow bus station on the start of its journey towards Barkingside Tesco on route 275. (Liam Farrer-Beddall)

Another Arriva London North route to cross the River Thames is the 168, which runs between Hampstead Heath and Old Kent Road Tesco, crossing the river via Waterloo Bridge. VLW132 (LJ03 MHE) is seen passing Euston station heading towards its southern terminus. (Liam Farrer-Beddall)

Route 253 (Euston station–Hackney Central) uses the forecourt of Clapton garage as its terminus at the northern end. VLW153 (LJ03 MDF) is seen having departed the Hackney Central stop. The road in the background of this photograph is now pedestrianised. (Liam Farrer-Beddall)

VLW172 (LJ03 MOV) is captured by the camera loading under the Finsbury Park rail bridges. VLW172 was one of a number of London buses that received all-over advertisements in 2012, promoting various sponsors of the London 2012 Olympic Games. It is seen promoting the Samsung Galaxy III mobile phone. (Liam Farrer-Beddall)

The last batch of VLWs arrived at Tottenham during the summer of 2003 to replace the DLA class. VLW190 (LJ03 MXR) is seen on layover amongst the rail bridges at Waterloo. VLW190 is another to show off the original Arriva 'cow horn' livery. (David Beddall)

A trio of Wright Eclipse Gemini-bodied Volvo B7TLs were purchased by London United in January 2002. Given the VR class code, they were intended for Hounslow but instead put to service from Fulwell. They then transferred to Shepherd's Bush in August 2003 before entering service on the 9 from Stamford Brook. VR228 (BD51 YCT) is seen on layover at Hammersmith bus station having travelled in from Aldwych. These three were the only Eclipse Geminis to be taken into stock by London United. (David Beddall)

The London General division of Go-Ahead London received their first Wright Eclipse Gemini-bodied Volvo B7TLs in 2002. WVL1 to WVL13 were allocated to Stockwell garage for route 345. WVL2 (LG02 KGU) is seen parked at Aldwych having completed a journey on the 87 from Wandsworth. The Go-Ahead London livery originally featured a grey skirt with yellow band as can be seen in this view. (Liam Farrer-Beddall)

Putney garage received the next fifty-eight WVL-class B7TLs (WVL14–71) and were allocated to routes 74 and 430. WVL36 (LF52 ZRU) is seen at Marble Arch whilst heading towards Baker Street station on route 74. (Liam Farrer-Beddall)

In the early 2000s, Putney High Street became a hotspot for the Gemini model, with a large number being allocated to Putney garage. WVL47 (LF52 ZRG) is seen travelling down the aforementioned Putney High Street heading for Warren Street on route 14. The WVL class replaced Routemasters on this service, as well as route 22. The WVL seen on the right of the photograph is heading for Putney garage itself. (Liam Farrer-Beddall)

Fifty WVL-class B7TLs were allocated to Stockwell garage over the first few months of 2003. WVL74 (LF52 ZPO) was delivered to the company in January 2003. It is captured by the camera at Tooting Broadway. It is seen blinded for its return journey on the 333 to Elephant & Castle. (David Beddall)

WVL103 (LF52 ZMO) was one of eighty-eight Gemini-bodied Volvo B7TLs allocated to Stockwell garage over the course of 2003. In November 2007 it left Stockwell for Mandela Way. It is photographed passing through Peckham whilst operating the 36 towards Queens Park. Note the lack of fleet names applied to this vehicle. (Liam Farrer-Beddall)

Thirty Volvo B7TLs were delivered to London General for the conversion of route 11 from Routemasters to low-floor buses. Some of the batch initially gained route branding as shown on WVL122 (LX53 AZP). It is seen travelling through Victoria bound for Liverpool Street station. (Liam Farrer-Beddall)

London and the south-east saw significant snow over the winter of 2010. This is shown in this view of WVL129 (LX53 AZA), which is seen passing through Aldwych in heavy snowfall. It can just be made out that it is operating the 87 towards Wandsworth when photographed. (Liam Farrer-Beddall)

February 2004 saw WVL148 (LX53 AYZ) gain an orange-based all-over advertisement for the West End show *The Lion King*, retaining this livery for a number of years. It is seen showing off this livery in Buckingham Palace Road passing Victoria coach station. (Liam Farrer-Beddall)

Northumberland Park garage finds a pair of Wright Eclipse Gemini-bodied Volvo B7TLs. On the left is WVL189 (LX05 FBC), new to Putney garage in 2005. It transferred to Northumberland Park in October 2012. On the right of the photograph is WVL79 (LF52 ZPK), a much-travelled B7TL. This latter vehicle has operated on three occasions from this garage. It was first allocated to Northumberland Park in the spring of 2013, before moving to Merton and Peckham, returning in January 2014. After leaving for a second time in May 2014, it found its way back in July 2016 and remained there until withdrawal in March 2018. It is captured by the camera a month later. (Aethan Blake)

Fifty-two Gemini-bodied Volvo B7TLs were purchased by London General in 2005 to replace Routemasters on routes 14 and 22. WVL204 (LX05 EZA) represents the batch. In November 2012, it moved to Northumberland Park and it is from this garage it operated route 257 between Stratford and Walthamstow Central. It is seen at Stratford bus station about to start its journey to Walthamstow. Upon refurbishment the WVLs lost their red and grey skirt livery in favour of 100 per cent red. (Liam Farrer-Beddall)

The winter of 2014 and 2015 saw twenty-two WVLs move to Metrobus' Green Street Green garage for operation in south-east London. WVL214 (LX06 DYU) is seen loading at Bromley South heading for Catford on route 320. This was new to London Central for routes 68 and 468. (Liam Farrer-Beddall)

London Central received their first and only new batch of Wright Eclipse Gemini-bodied Volvo B7TLs in 2006. Sixty-two of them were allocated to Camberwell where they were shared between routes 68, N68, X68 and 468. WVL230 (LX06 DZN) is seen at Elephant & Castle starting its journey south to South Croydon. (Liam Farrer-Beddall)

The sixty-two-strong fleet of WVLs at Camberwell garage found use on the garages other double-deck services including the 45 (Kings Cross–Clapham Park). WVL245 (LX06 EAG) is seen about to pass Kings Cross station. (Liam Farrer-Beddall)

Although slightly out of sequence, WVL239 (LX06 DZY) was one of a handful of original Volvo B7TLs that were still in use in south London during 2020. It is operating route 127, passing through a busy Mitcham. A brief comparison can be made with the Wright Eclipse Gemini 3, an example of which can be seen behind WVL239. (Liam Farrer-Beddall)

East Thames Buses took stock of two batches of Wright Eclipse Gemini-bodied Volvo B7TLs. The first thirty-one were ordered for route 180 at Belvedere. VWL20 (LF52 TGX) represents this batch, seen crossing Waterloo Bridge. It is photographed operating service 1 between Russell Square and Canada Water. (Liam Farrer-Beddall)

Thirteen additional VWL-class B7TLs were taken into stock during 2004 to replace the last of the Volvo Olympians at East Thames Buses. These were also initially used on the 180 and 185. VWL44 (BX04 BKJ) represents the batch, and is seen attending the Showbus 2006 rally held at the Imperial War Museum, Duxford. (Liam Farrer-Beddall)

In late 2003 to early 2004 First London changed from the Plaxton President to the Wright Eclipse Gemini for its double-deck fleet. First London went on to purchase a number of both the Gemini and Gemini 2 models. The first arrived between December 2003 and February 2004 at Alperton originally for the 92. VNZ32343 (LK53 LZO) is seen passing Wembley Stadium heading for Ealing Hospital. (Liam Farrer-Beddall)

Alperton's route 79 (Alperton–Edgware) also received some of the first Gemini-bodied Volvo B7TLs with First London in early 2004. VNW32353 (LK53 LZR) is seen at journey's end in Alperton before setting off on its journey to Edgware. (David Beddall)

In July 2012 eleven Wright Eclipse Gemini-bodied Volvo B7TLs were transferred to Lea Interchange garage to double-deck route 308 during the London 2012 Olympic Games. VNW32356 (LK53 LZV) was one of this batch and is seen passing the Eaton Manor Transport Hub located close to Lea Interchange garage. (Liam Farrer-Beddall)

The largest batch of Wright Eclipse Geminis purchased by First London arrived over the summer of 2004. They were shared between routes 28, 31 and 328 and were allocated to Westbourne Park. VNW32366 (LK04 HYY) is seen at Shepherd's Bush in the 100 per cent red livery. (Liam Farrer-Beddall)

Notting Hill Gate saw all three routes (28, 31 and 328) pass through. VNW32419 (LK04 JCU) is seen at this location heading towards Chelsea, World's End, wearing the all-red livery. (David Beddall)

Members of the batch allocated to Westbourne Park often found themselves off their intended routes. VNW32426 (LK04 HYF) is seen operating route 23 to Liverpool Street, passing through Trafalgar Square. It shows off the original First London livery. (Liam Farrer-Beddall)

The final nine Geminis were allocated to First London's Rainham and later Dagenham garages and put to use on the 150. VNW32661 (LK55 AAJ) is captured by the camera at Ilford Broadway. (Liam Farrer-Beddall)

Travel London took stock of their first Wright Eclipse Gemini-bodied Volvo B7TLs in September 2004. In October 2009, they transferred to Abellio London. The first of the batch, 9001 (BX54 DHJ), is seen at Stratford International on rail replacement duties. (Liam Farrer-Beddall)

9035 (BX55 XMJ) is seen loading in Peckham town centre. It is operating a journey on the 343 to New Cross Gate. The Abellio fleet name can be seen clearly in this photograph. (Liam Farrer-Beddall)

Travel London purchased V21 to V65 to cover the PVR requirements on routes 185 and 343. They were later renumbered 9021 to 9065. 9054 (BX55 XNG) is seen exiting Canada Water bus station whilst operating route 381 to Peckham. 9054 was originally numbered V54 by its former operator. (Liam Farrer-Beddall)

A handful of Geminis were used on route 157 in south-west London. 9067 (BX55 XNW) is seen on layover at Morden station. The Travel London logo was similar to that of parent company Travel West Midlands. (Liam Farrer-Beddall)

The demise of First London in 2013 saw the majority of Eclipse Geminis transfer to Tower Transit. They retained their former First London fleet numbers. VNW32389 (LK04 HZX) is seen heading towards Westbourne Park on route 23. Aldwych provides the backdrop to this photograph. (Liam Farrer-Beddall)

Arriva London ordered fifty Wright Eclipse Pulsar-bodied VDL DB250s for north London routes 242 and 253 from Clapton garage. However, this never went ahead, and they were reallocated to Arriva London South. They were used on services around the Croydon area. DW1 is seen at East Croydon operating route 194 to nearby West Croydon. In June 2004 it lost its original registration mark, LJ03 MWM, in favour of cherished registration mark 801 DYE. (Liam Farrer-Beddall)

DW25 (725 DYE) was another allocated to Croydon. It also gained its cherished registration in June 2004. It shows the original Arriva London livery and dual-door layout. New Addington provides the location of this photograph. (Liam Farrer-Beddall)

Brixton garage was next to receive a batch of DW-class Wright Eclipse Pulsars. They arrived in March and April 2004, and were used mainly on the 137. DW58 (LJ04 LFD) is seen passing Marble Arch, followed by a Plaxton President, one of the competitors of the Gemini and Pulsar models. (Liam Farrer-Beddall)

Another of the Brixton allocation, DW83 (LJ04 LFW), is seen travelling down a busy Park Lane operating a shorter journey to Marble Arch on route 137. (Liam Farrer-Beddall)

DW103 to DW134 were allocated to the Battersea outstation of Brixton in March and April 2005. They were used on the 19 between Finsbury Park and Battersea Bridge (South Side). The first of the batch, DW103 (LJ05 BJV), is seen parked at Finsbury Park station before heading back to south London. (David Beddall)

The loss of route 19 in 2012 allowed the batch of DWs used on the route to be refurbished. They were then employed on London 2012 Olympic work over the summer in an all-red unidentifiable livery. DW114 (LJ05 DHX) is seen departing the Eaton Manor Transport Hub on Olympic duties. Note the blue security tape applied to opening parts of buses used on this type of work. (Liam Farrer-Beddall)

Seven Wright Eclipse Pulsar-bodied VDL DB250 double-decks were purchased by Arriva Kent Thameside for use on the 492 between Bluewater, Bexleyheath and Sidcup station. They were delivered to Dartford garage in December 2003 and January 2004, before entering service at the end of the month. 6213 (GK53 AOA) is captured by the camera passing through Bexleyheath town centre bound for Sidcup station. (Liam Farrer-Beddall)

Eleven Wright Eclipse Pulsars were delivered to Arriva The Shires and allocated to Garston garage. They were put to use on the 258 (South Harrow–Watford Junction) but were also used on Garston's other Transport for London services 142 and 340. Edgware finds 6029 (YJ55 WOC), which is seen heading north to Watford Junction on route 142. (Liam Farrer-Beddall)

Go Ahead London took a pair of integral Wright Eclipse Gemini 2 models in December 2008, a hybrid and a diesel version. The hybrid version took stock number WHD1, registered LX58 CWJ. It was allocated to Stockwell garage and used mostly on the 196. However, it is photographed at Victoria having a day out on the 24 (Pimlico–Hampstead Heath). Although it was a Gemini 2 model, it carried the styling of the original Gemini model. It returned to Wrightbus, Ballymena, during March 2012. (Liam Farrer-Beddall)

The diesel version of the Gemini 2 integral model was initially allocated to Camberwell garage, but unlike the hybrid version it received the Gemini 2 front end. WDL1 (LX58 GWG) was essentially a replacement for WVL221, which was destroyed by fire in March 2008. Arriving in London during January 2009, it remained in London service until 2019, outlasting WHD1. It is seen negotiating Trafalgar Square whilst operating service 88. (Liam Farrer-Beddall)

First London took stock of ten integral Gemini 2s in early 2009, five hybrids and five diesels. Westbourne Park received both batches for route 328. WNH39005 (LK58 ECZ) represents the hybrid version; the green leaf livery can be seen, with appropriate branding on the front of the vehicle. It is photographed passing through Notting Hill Gate bound for Chelsea, World's End. (David Beddall)

First London also took stock of five diesel integrals in January and February 2009. Like the hybrid versions, they were allocated to Westbourne Park where they were allocated to route 328. They could also be found operating other routes from that garage including the 23. WN35003 (LK58 EDR) is seen approaching Trafalgar Square whilst on the 23. (Liam Farrer-Beddall)

The final integral Wrightbus Gemini 2s to arrive in London put in an appearance in late 2008 to early 2009 with Arriva London. They were allocated to Wood Green garage where they were compared against the Volvo B5LH model, which will feature later. HW3 (LJ58 AVK) is seen in Wood Green heading towards Palmers Green, having travelled from London Bridge on the 141. The batch originally carried the green leaf livery. (Liam Farrer-Beddall)

The first six Volvo B5LHs were also put to use on the 141 and compared with the HW class integrals. Although the HWs entered service before the HVs, the latter class gained the older-style front end. This is shown by HV4 (LJ09 KOH), which is seen in full green leaf livery. The Hollywood Cinema in Wood Green can be seen in the background, with HV4 having completed its journey on route 243. (Liam Farrer-Beddall)

Arriva London took stock of the first production batch of the integral Gemini 2s. This model featured parts from VDL and became known as the VDL DB300. Arriva were the only company to take stock of the type, with other operators taking a preference for the Volvo B9TL or B5LH model. No less than seventy-nine of the type arrived over the course of 2009 at Clapton garage to replace the Mercedes-Benz Citaro bendy buses on the 38, and to convert route 242 to the type. DW209 (LJ09 SVD) is seen passing the entrance to Clapton garage whilst heading towards Victoria on route 38. (David Beddall)

In 2014 route 38 was converted to the LT-class New Bus for London type, at which time the DWs were reallocated within the Arriva London group. Many operated from a number of garages including DW237 (LJ59 AEG), which was passed between Brixton, Norwood and Ash Grove garages before settling down at Grays. The former Arriva Southern Counties garage, now under control of Arriva London, gained a number of TfL contracts in the Romford area during 2017. DW237 is seen about to pass Romford station. (Liam Farrer-Beddall)

The 38 was a frequent service which often caused bunching on the service as can be seen in this view of DW242 (LJ59 ACU). It is seen passing Green Park on its approach to Hyde Park Corner. A Routemaster on the heritage 9H service can also be seen in this view. (Liam Farrer-Beddall)

Brixton garage was next to receive the DW-class DB300 model. Eighteen were allocated to the garage to convert route 59 (Streatham, Telford Avenue–Kings Cross). DW295 (LJ59 LWA) is seen reaching journey's end at Kings Cross followed by a DAF DB250 DLA class also operating the 59. (Liam Farrer-Beddall)

DW307 (LJ10 CVP) was one of thirty-nine Gemini 2-bodied DB300s allocated to Tottenham garage in 2010 for the conversion of bendy bus route 149 (London Bridge–Edmonton Green). 2017 saw the conversion of the 149 to the New Routemaster LT class. After this, the majority of DWs moved to Croydon for further use. It is at this location that we find DW307 operating a journey on the 60 to Old Coulsdon. (Liam Farrer-Beddall)

DW313 (LJ10 CUY) is seen at the southern end of route 149, about to enter London Bridge station. It has just crossed London Bridge itself, which can be seen in the background. DW313 is followed by a WVL-class Volvo B9TL operating a journey on the 21 to Lewisham, and another DW on the 149. (Liam Farrer-Beddall)

Another of the original 149 batch of Gemini 2s is seen in use from Croydon garage. This time, DW315 (LJ10 CVB) is seen passing through Penge bound for West Croydon on the 194. (Liam Farrer-Beddall)

DW334 (LJ60 AXT) is seen close to its home garage in Tottenham. It is heading towards London Bridge. An ALX400 can be seen peaking behind the DW. Like the 38, the 149 was another route to be converted to the LT-class New Routemaster type, after which the DWs moved around the Arriva London group as required. (Liam Farrer-Beddall)

Two months after it was delivered to Arriva London in May 2011, DW411 (LJ11 AEB) suffered a fire in July of that year. It returned to Northern Ireland during the same month where it remained for over a year. It finally returned to London in January 2013 featuring an extended rear overhang which accommodated a new Euro 6 engine. Although it returned to London in January 2013, it went to the Millbrook testing ground in Bedfordshire, returning to Wright in June 2013 before finally re-entering service the same month. It is seen entering Edmonton Green bus station. (Liam Farrer-Beddall)

The original batch of DWs purchased for the 38 and 242 at Clapton were supported by a fleet of ADL Enviro 400s. In 2011 Arriva London purchased an additional twenty-seven DWs to replace these Enviro 400s. DW424 (LJ11 ACZ) was part of this batch, which in turn got replaced by a fleet of Gemini 3s in 2017. After this, they were redeployed to Dartford for use on newly gained contracts in south-east London. DW424 is photographed approaching the northern end of Bromley town centre, before terminating at Bromley North station. The 269 operates between the latter destination and Bexleyheath. (Liam Farrer-Beddall)

Thirty-seven DWs were allocated to Stamford Hill garage to replace the bendy buses on the 73 in August and September 2011. DW436 (LJ11 ABO) is one of the batch and is seen shortly after entering service, rounding Marble Arch. (Liam Farrer-Beddall)

Early in 2013 the 73 batch moved from Stamford Hill to Tottenham, after which time they could be seen on any of the routes from that garage. DW440 (LJ11 ABZ) demonstrates this, operating a journey on the 243. (Liam Farrer-Beddall)

Another example of the DWs intended for the 73 being off route is seen here in this photograph. The 243 stands at Tenyson Way, Waterloo, before heading back to Wood Green. The Shard can be viewed above the centre area of DW448 (LJ61 CFL). (Liam Farrer-Beddall)

Arriva London's final bendy bus route, the 29 (Wood Green–Trafalgar Square) lost its bendy buses during 2011 when more DWs were purchased to replace them. DW475 (LJ61 CBX) is seen rounding Trafalgar Square embarking on its return journey to Wood Green. (Liam Farrer-Beddall)

The batch of DWs allocated to the 29 mostly stayed true to the service, although they were sometimes used on other routes from Wood Green. DW484 (LJ61 CCU) demonstrates this, photographed on layover at Edgware station whilst operating the 221. DW290 can be seen parked behind. (Liam Farrer-Beddall)

DW499 to DW515 were also allocated to Wood Green and were intended to operate routes 141 and 144. However, they were often used on the 29 as seen here. Trafalgar Square finds DW499 (LJ62 BKD) about to head north to Wood Green shortly after its arrival in the capital. (Liam Farrer-Beddall)

In 2013 Arriva London won three routes from Stagecoach London, the 67, 106 and 230. The company chose the DW class for the take up of these services. DW516 to DW533 were new to the 106 (Whitechapel–Finsbury Park station). The latter location finds DW518 (LJ13 CCZ). (Liam Farrer-Beddall)

Routes 67 and 230 were both operated from Tottenham garage. Twenty-two DWs were shared between the two services. DW535 (LJ13 CLO) is captured by the camera departing Walthamstow Central whilst operating route 230 to Upper Walthamstow. (Liam Farrer-Beddall)

DW555 (LJ13 CEK) was the last of the batch originally allocated to Tottenham for the 67 and 230. In February 2018 it transferred to Ponders End where it joined similar vehicles operating the 121. It is seen passing through Wood Green town centre sporting an all-over advertisement for Transport for London, promoting unlimited bus journeys for £1.50 within an hour. (Liam Farrer-Beddall)

Ponders End garage operates route 121 between Enfield and Turnpike Lane station. Over the course of spring 2013 the rolling stock on the route was renewed with twenty-three DWs. The route passes through Southgate station, and it is this station that provides the backdrop to this photograph of DW565 (LJ13 CKE). (Liam Farrer-Beddall)

The final batch of eight DWs were allocated to Tottenham garage and officially allocated to route 41. However, they were again used on other services such as the 230. The final DW to be delivered, DW586 (LT63 UKH), is seen waiting at traffic lights exiting Walthamstow Central bus station bound for Wood Green on route 230. (Liam Farrer-Beddall)

An increase in TfL work in 2009 led Arriva The Shires to purchase a pair of Gemini 2-bodied DB300 double-decks, both of which were allocated to Garston. 6101 (KX59 AEF) represents the pair. It is seen departing Brent Cross bound for Watford Junction on route 142. In 2016 the pair joined the main Arriva London fleet, being renumbered DW190 and DW191 respectively. (Liam Farrer-Beddall)

First London took stock of the first Volvo B9TLs in London, with thirty-one of the type entering service from Alperton garage on the 83 between Ealing Hospital and Golders Green. VN37773 (LK59 CWN) was numerically the first of the large number of B9TLs purchased by First London. It is seen on Wembley High Road bound for Golders Green. (Liam Farrer-Beddall)

Golders Green bus station finds VN37777 (LK59 CWT), another of the thirty-one strong batch purchased by First London in 2009 for the 83. This batch of vehicles passed to Metroline in June 2013 when First made its exit from the capital. (Liam Farrer-Beddall)

The next batch of B9TLs were allocated to Northumberland Park to be shared between the 259 and 476. However, Walthamstow Central finds VN37811 (LK59 FEF) off route, operating the 357 towards Whipps Cross. (Liam Farrer-Beddall)

VN37813 (LK59 FEH) is seen on one of its intended services, the 259 (Kings Cross–Edmonton Green). It is at the latter destination where it is captured by the camera. It is being followed by a DW-class Gemini 2-bodied DB300 from Arriva London. (Liam Farrer-Beddall)

Before changes to bus services in central London the 259 and 476 would meet on the eastern side of Kings Cross station, the junction which can be seen in the background of this photograph. The 476 would then carry on past Kings Cross and St Pancras to reach its terminus at Euston station. Kings Cross station building itself can be seen to the left of VN37826 (LK59 FDU), which is seen heading to Euston. (Liam Farrer-Beddall)

Lea Interchange garage received sixteen Volvo B9TLs in February 2010 for use on the 58 between East Ham and Walthamstow Central. VN37830 (BG59 FXD) is seen starting its journey to East Ham leaving Walthamstow Central. Another of the type can be glimpsed in the background. (Liam Farrer-Beddall)

Northumberland Park garage received a further twenty-two B9TLs in March 2010 to complete the conversion of the 259 and 476 to the type. Tottenham is another area where the 259 and 476 meets and it is at this location that we find VN37853 (BV10 WWL) heading towards Euston. (Liam Farrer-Beddall)

Edmonton Green bus station provides the northern terminus of the 259. As the sign to the left of VN37861 (BV10 WWU) suggests, this is the location of this photograph. (Liam Farrer-Beddall)

First London's Hayes garage took delivery of twenty-four Volvo B9TLs during April and May 2010 for use on the 427 (Acton High Street–Uxbridge station). VN37874 (BK10 MFN) is seen departing Uxbridge for its journey to Acton. (Liam Farrer-Beddall)

VN37878 (BF10 LSU) was another of the batch allocated to Hayes garage for the 427. It is seen shortly after being delivered to London, about to enter Uxbridge station. (Liam Farrer-Beddall)

The largest batch of B9TLs to be taken into stock by First London was for the replacement of bendy buses on the 18. Fifty-three of the type were allocated to Willesden Junction. VN37894 (BF60 UUC) is seen passing through Wembley Central heading to Sudbury. (Liam Farrer-Beddall)

London buses are also regularly used on rail replacement work at weekends. One of the route 18 batch, VN37916 (BF60 VHW), is seen out of its normal area of operation at Canning Town station. (Liam Farrer-Beddall)

Route 18 runs on the northern edge of central London to reach Euston station. VN37928 (BF60 VJD) is seen passing along Euston Road before returning to Sudbury. (Liam Farrer-Beddall)

June 2011 saw routes 25, 26 and 30 pass from Stagecoach to First London, all operating from Lea Interchange. Route 25 gained sixty-five Volvo B9TLs, replacing bendy buses on the 25. VN36107 (BJ11 DTY) is seen heading towards Ilford at Bow Church. (Liam Farrer-Beddall)

VN36152 (BJ11 EAE) is another of the batch purchased for the 25. It is seen heading towards Oxford Circus through Stratford Broadway. Until recently, the southbound journeys on the 25 never served the Stratford bus station. (Liam Farrer-Beddall)

A modest batch of eight Volvo B9TLs were allocated to Northumberland Park in February 2012 for use on route 357. VN37949 (BL61 ADO) is seen leaving Walthamstow Central bound for Whipps Cross. (Liam Farrer-Beddall)

VN37952 to VN37984 were allocated to Westbourne Park garage for use on the 23 until a batch of Enviro 400s arrived in 2012. They also saw service on other Westbourne Park double-deck services including the 295. VN37954 (BN61 MKX) is seen here heading back to Ladbrooke Grove Sainsbury's having just left its Clapham Junction terminus. (Liam Farrer-Beddall)

In 2012 First London was successful in winning the tender for the 266 (Hammersmith–Brent Cross). The Volvo B9TL was again the chosen type for the route. The batch put to use temporarily on the 23 were the intended batch for the 266, but five top-up vehicles were also purchased. One of these, VN36294 (BX12 CVL), is seen on its way to Hammersmith at Harlesden. Sister vehicle VN36292 is seen passing in the opposite direction. (Liam Farrer-Beddall)

The final batch of Volvo B9TLs to arrive with First London were allocated to Westbourne Park. They were put to use on the 295 between Clapham Junction and Ladbrooke Grove Sainsbury's. Clapham Junction finds VN37993 (BF62 UYD) departing for Ladbrooke Grove. (Liam Farrer-Beddall)

Go-Ahead London was the second operator to take stock of Wright Eclipse Gemini 2-bodied Volvo B9TL. The first twenty-nine were allocated to London Central's New Cross garage and used on the 21 between Lewisham and Newington Green. WVL286 (LX59 CZC) is seen off route in Lewisham heading towards Foots Cray on the 321. (Liam Farrer-Beddall)

Route 21 crosses the River Thames using London Bridge. WVL281 (LX59 CYW) is seen heading south to Lewisham having just crossed this bridge, and is about to pass the entrance to London Bridge station. (Liam Farrer-Beddall)

The next thirty-one were also allocated to London Central, this time to Peckham garage. They were used on the 63 between Honor Oak and Kings Cross. WVL304 (LX59 CYC) is seen about to cross Ludgate Circus heading towards Kings Cross. (Liam Farrer-Beddall)

The St Pancras Hotel provides the backdrop to this photograph of WVL330 (LX59 DDK). The 63 terminated on York Way, Kings Cross, before travelling to the other side of St Pancras to start its journey. (Liam Farrer-Beddall)

Blue Triangle won the contract for the East London Transit services in the Ilford and Barking areas. Sixteen WVLs were taken into stock at Rainham in February 2010. Split between routes EL1 and EL2, WVL334 to WVL349 wore the distinctive livery shown above, along with East London Transit branding. WVL337 LX59DDU is about to pass through Barking town centre on its way to Dagenham Dock. (Liam Farrer-Beddall)

In 2017 a number of the former East London Transit WVLs underwent a complete refurbishment, losing the centre exit doors and being fitted with luggage racks for use on the X26 between West Croydon and Heathrow Central. One such vehicle was WVL344 (LX59 DFD), which is seen at East Croydon showing its conversion. (Liam Farrer-Beddall)

The opening months of 2011 saw WVL350 to WVL385 allocated to Bexleyheath for use on routes 229 and 422. WVL356 (LX60 DWF) is seen on the forecourt of Bexleyheath garage. The single-deck routes in the Bexleyheath area were also renewed at the same time. (Liam Farrer-Beddall)

London Central's New Cross garage received a batch of Volvo B9TLs for use on the 171 in April 2011. They were also put to use on other double-deck services from this garage including the 36. WVL388 (LX11 CVN) is seen on this service passing Marble Arch bound for Queen's Park. (Liam Farrer-Beddall)

WVL402 (LX11 CWE) was one of the twenty-seven-strong fleet of WVLs allocated to London Central's New Cross garage in 2011. It is seen entering Southampton Row from Aldwych before completing its journey to Holborn on route 171. (Liam Farrer-Beddall)

Go-Ahead London's Docklands Buses subsidiary received a batch of Volvo B7TLs in 2011, which they shared between routes 474 and D7, allocated to Silvertown. WVL414 (LX11 CWV) is seen at Canning Town station on route 474 towards Manor Park. (Liam Farrer-Beddall)

Route 12 lost its bendy buses during the autumn of 2011 in favour of the WVL-class Volvo B9TL. Twenty of the type were allocated to Camberwell for the route. Route 12 received a batch of New Routemasters in 2015, after which time the WVLs found other work. November 2016 saw WVL445 (LJ61 GWD) redeployed to Sutton. It is photographed at the Putney Bridge terminus of route 93. (Liam Farrer-Beddall)

WVL455 and WVL456 were ordered by Go-Ahead London against the tender win for school route 658. They were, however, used on other duties from their home garage, Bexleyheath. The first of the pair, WVL455 (LJ61 GYP), is seen whilst working on London 2012 Olympic Games work exiting the Eaton Manor Transport hub that was set up close to Lea Interchange garage. (Liam Farrer-Beddall)

2012 saw further deliveries of the B9TL to the Go-Ahead London group for various contracts won by the company. Route 20 (Walthamstow Central–Debden) gained a small batch of the type during February and March 2012, shortly followed by a batch for the 249 in south London. WVL465 (LJ61 NVA) is seen setting out on its journey to Debden at Walthamstow. (Liam Farrer-Beddall)

March 2012 saw First London sell its Northumberland Park garage to Go-Ahead London. Included in the sale were fifty-three Wright Eclipse Gemini 2-bodied Volvo B9TLs, which gained the class code WVN. WVN21 (LK59 FDO) was one of these vehicles, and is seen at journey's end making its way to its stand at Euston station, which can just be seen to the left of the picture. (Liam Farrer-Beddall)

The last batch of thirteen Volvo B9TLs for the Go-Ahead London group were intended to enter service on the 22 from Putney garage. However, most found work on the 74 instead. This is illustrated by WVL501 (LJ62 KZD), which is seen at Marble Arch bound for Baker Street station. (Liam Farrer-Beddall)

Metroline took stock of their first Volvo B9TLs between January and March 2010. The former Armchair garage at Brentford were the first to take stock of the type, which gained the class code VW when they upgraded the rolling stock on the 237 (White City–Hounslow Heath). VW1034 (LK59 JJU) is seen in Hounslow bound for White City. VW1034 was the only 59-plate VW to be purchased new by Metroline. (Liam Farrer-Beddall)

Brentford received the second batch of VWs in the autumn of 2010, this time for the E2 Ealing local service. The first of this batch, VW1056 (LK60 AEA) is seen rounding Shepherd's Bush Green heading towards White City on the 237. (Liam Farrer-Beddall)

Unlike First London and Go-Ahead London, Metroline took a more modest number of Volvo B9TLs into stock. The next batch to arrive didn't do so until May and June 2011 when Perivale received a batch for the 105 (Greenford station–Heathrow Central). VW1184 (LK11 CXU) represents this batch and is seen in Greenford Broadway, completing the short journey to nearby Greenford station. (Liam Farrer-Beddall)

These were soon followed by another batch for Edgware garage. VW1193 to VW1216 were put to use on the 79. VW1195 (LK11 CYL) is seen entering Edgware station. A comparison between the Gemini 2's main rival, the Enviro 400, can be made with the TE-class seen behind. (Liam Farrer-Beddall)

2012 saw the arrival of no less than sixty-four VW-class B9TLs with Metroline, all of which being allocated to Holloway. They were shared between routes 43, 134 and W7 but were also found on other double-deck routes from that garage. VW1252 (LK12 ACZ) is seen on layover at the Tottenham Court Road stand on route 134. (David Beddall)

As mentioned in the previous caption the large batch of VWs at Holloway could often be found off their intended route. This was the case when VW1280 (LK12 AMO) was captured by the camera at Marble Arch. On this occasion it was deputising for a New Bus for London on the 390. (Liam Farrer-Beddall)

Out of the 43, 134 and W7, the W7 (Finsbury Park–Muswell Hill) has the smallest vehicle requirement of the three services. VW1288 (LK12 AOY) is seen negotiating the bus parking area at Muswell Hill setting off for its journey back to Finsbury Park. (David Beddall)

The final batch of new VWs to be taken into stock by Metroline were allocated to Willesden garage from where they operated the 52 service to Victoria. VW1393 (LK62 DUU) is seen passing through Notting Hill Gate. (Liam Farrer-Beddall)

In June 2013 Metroline acquired part of the First London operation in west London, taking control of garages at Hayes, Greenford, Willesden Junction, Uxbridge and Alperton. With this operation came a large number of vehicles including 120 Wright Eclipse Gemini 2-bodied Volvo B9TLs. VW1754 (LK59 CWP) represents this large batch, and was allocated to Alperton. It is seen arriving at Edgware station. (Liam Farrer-Beddall)

In July 2019 Metroline was successful in winning the contract for route 81 between Hounslow and Slough, a route that had been operated for many years by London United. For this operation, a new garage was established at the former Westbus site in the Hounslow area, which gained garage code 'SG'. VW1403 (LK62 DVR) was one of the vehicles transferred to this new operation. It is seen in a wet Slough bus station having just completed its journey from Hounslow. (Liam Farrer-Beddall)

Arriva London did not purchase any new examples of the Volvo B9TL model. However, in October 2017 ten B9TLs were acquired by Arriva London to replace older VLA-class Volvo B7TLs on the 123 between Wood Green and Ilford, numbered VLW901–10. VLW902 (BN61 MXW) was new to First London as VN37973, and passed to Tower Transit in June 2013. It is photographed at Stratford bus station on route 158 in July 2020. The Covid-19 pandemic of 2020–21 saw a reduction in the seating capacity allowed on buses, not only in London but around the UK. Double-decks were restricted to carrying around thirty people, this being displayed by the notice on the entrance doors. (Liam Farrer-Beddall)

Golden Tours have operated a number of Volvo B9TLs over the course of its history, mainly carrying MCV bodywork. However, in May 2012 the company purchased a solitary Wright Eclipse Gemini 2 version. It was put to use on the shuttle service the company operates between London Victoria and the Harry Potter Studio Tour in Leavesden, Watford. It is photographed at this latter location loading before setting off back to London. (Liam Farrer-Beddall)

London City Tours did not last long on the London Sightseeing tour scene. However, the company purchased a handful of former Metroline and Go-Ahead London Volvo B9TLs for the 2018 season. Former Go-Ahead London WVL371 (LX60 DXB) was converted to full open-top layout. It is seen negotiating Trafalgar Square, followed by a Golden Tours Volvo B5TL. (Liam Farrer-Beddall)

Arriva London took stock of the first Wright Eclipse Gemini 2-bodied Volvo B5LHs in London. The company had trialled five of the type alongside a batch of Wrightbus integral hybrid buses. Twenty-one B5LHs were purchased and allocated to Tottenham garage, from where they were used on the 76, arriving in November and December 2010. Spring 2017 saw the original batch transfer south to Brixton for use on the 133. HV17 (LJ60 AWH) represents this batch and is loading just before crossing the River Thames using London Bridge. (Liam Farrer-Beddall)

The next batch of twenty HV-class Volvo B5LH double-deckers arrived with Arriva London between June and August 2011, entering service on the 73 in September. These vehicles operated alongside a batch of DW-class Geminis on the route until the following year when further HVs were taken into stock. HV39 (LJ11 EFK) is seen making its way to Stoke Newington whilst operating route 67. (Liam Farrer-Beddall)

In August 2016, Arriva London painted HV64 (WLT 664) into a platinum-based livery to celebrate 1,000 award-winning Arriva London staff. It is captured by the camera in Wood Green, heading for London Bridge on route 141. (Liam Farrer-Beddall)

November and December 2012 saw a further thirty-five Gemini 2-bodied Volvo B5LHs taken into stock by Arriva London, completing the allocation of the HV class on route 73. HV78 (LJ62 BGZ) is seen passing through Marble Arch whilst heading north to Stoke Newington. The subtle hybrid logos applied to the batch can just be glimpsed ahead of the rear wheel arch. (Liam Farrer-Beddall)

No less than forty-eight HV-class Volvo B5LHs were taken into stock by Arriva London between April and June 2013, converting route 29 (Wood Green–Trafalgar Square) to the type. HV98 (LJ13 FCY) represents this large batch, travelling through Holloway Road towards Trafalgar Square. (Liam Farrer-Beddall)

Sister vehicle HV124 (LJ13 FAU) is seen heading towards Trafalgar Square on a fine summer's day. Charing Cross Road provides the backdrop to this photograph. (Liam Farrer-Beddall)

The final twenty-one Gemini 2-bodied B5LHs to be purchased by Arriva London arrived in January and February 2014. They were allocated to Brixton for use on the 319, but more often than not could be found on any of Brixton's double-deck services. Illustrating this is HV133 (LT63 UJO), seen at Waterloo operating the 59 to Kings Cross. Waterloo station can be seen on the right of the photograph. (Liam Farrer-Beddall)

Another example of the batch intended for the 319 is HV141 (LT63 UJY). It is photographed crossing London Bridge whilst operating route 133 to Streatham station. The City of London provides the backdrop to this photograph. (Liam Farrer-Beddall)

A smaller quantity of Gemini 2-bodied Volvo B5LHs were purchased by the Go-Ahead London group. The company allocated class code WHV to the type. London Central's Camberwell garage took stock of the first sixteen and used them, alongside Volvo B9TLs on the 12, replacing bendy buses on the route. WHV13 (LJ61 GXM) is captured by the camera in Lewisham, heading towards Battersea Park station on a shortened route 436. (Liam Farrer-Beddall)

Fifteen B5LHs arrived at Stockwell in March 2012 for the part-conversion of the 19, the numbers being made up by WVL-class Volvo B9TLs. After the loss of the 19 in 2017, during April and May the batch moved to Merton for use on the 131. WHV27 (LJ12 CHK) is seen off route at Tooting Broadway heading to Mitcham on the 270. (Liam Farrer-Beddall)

Another of the batch transferred to Merton to help with the takeover of route 131 (Kingston–Tooting Broadway) from London United. Featured slightly out of sequence in this book, WHV23 (LJ61 NVK) is seen about to pass Cromwell Road bus station in Kingston at the start of its journey to Tooting Broadway. (Liam Farrer-Beddall)

London General's Putney garage took stock of the last batch of Gemini 2-bodied B5LHs. Ten WHVs arrived in October and November 2012, ordered for the 22. However, the batch were used more on the 74 (Putney High Street–Baker Street) as demonstrated by WHV39 (LJ62 KHF). It is seen passing the access road to Putney Bridge Underground station, just before crossing Putney Bridge itself. (Liam Farrer-Beddall)

Metroline took a more modest quantity of the B5LH/Gemini 2 model, with seventeen vehicles of this combination being purchased. The first five were used on the 24 (Hampstead Heath–Pimlico), trialled against the Volvo B9TL model. They arrived in October 2012, and were operated from Holloway. One of each type can be seen in this view at the Hampstead Heath terminus, the main focus of the photograph being VWH1363 (LK62 DJZ). (Liam Farrer-Beddall)

Twelve additional VWHs were purchased by Metroline in January 2013 for use on the 52 (Victoria–Willesden Bus Garage), again working alongside VW-class B9TLs. VWH1415 (LK62 DWU) represents this batch, and is photographed passing through Notting Hill Gate. (David Beddall)

Under the ownership of Transdev, the new London Sovereign operation took stock of twenty-three Gemini 2-bodied Volvo B5LHs, which they classified VH. They were used to replace SLE-class Scania double-decks on the 13 (Aldwych–Golders Green). The first of the batch, VH1 (BD13 OHU), is seen passing Baker Street station on its way to Aldwych. (Liam Farrer-Beddall)

Another member of the batch, VH16 (BT13 YWM), is seen travelling along the Strand shortly before approaching its terminus at Aldwych. The new version of Transdev logos applied to the batch can clearly be seen in this photograph. Nelson's Column can also just be glimpsed on the right-hand side of the photograph. (Liam Farrer-Beddall)

March 2014 saw the London United and London Sovereign fleets reunited under the RATP-DEV Group. VH19 (BT13 YWR) is photographed at Harrow, heading to Golders Green on the 183. In 2016 VH19 was renumbered VH45119. The 13 was lost by Sovereign in 2017 to Tower Transit. (Liam Farrer-Beddall)

October 2013 saw Go-Ahead London take a Volvo B5TL demonstrator on loan. Registered BF63 HFE, it was allocated temporary fleet number V6. The vehicle featured a Euro 6 engine and a revised rear end, which would become a feature on the new Gemini 3 model. It is seen at Trafalgar Square heading towards Dulwich Library on route 12. (Liam Farrer-Beddall)

The first Eclipse Gemini 3 models to arrive in London came in the form of two demonstrators. Arriva London received one of these vehicles, which was numbered VGD1 (BF63 HDE). The original Gemini 3 had a similar front end to the Gemini 2 as can be seen above. VGD1 is seen on layover at Edgware before embarking on its journey back to Wood Green. (Liam Farrer-Beddall)

Between April and June 2014, Stagecoach London received thirty-two Eclipse Gemini 3-bodied Volvo B5LHs, the first batch to be taken into stock by a London operator. They were allocated to Plumstead garage from where they operated the 53 between Plumstead station and Whitehall, Horse Guards Parade. 13003 (BU14 EFY) is seen at Parliament Square, about to enter Whitehall for the final part of its journey. (Liam Farrer-Beddall)

The Gemini 3-bodied B5LHs lasted for five years with Stagecoach London before they were withdrawn, replaced by the standard AD Enviro 400 MMC model. After withdrawal, all thirty-two examples passed to Arriva London for further use in north London. 13007 (BN14 VZK) is seen parked up, withdrawn, at West Ham garage. (Aethan Blake)

The batch of B5TLs used on the 53 were also found operating other routes from Plumstead garage. Demonstrating this is 13014 (BN14 WAE), which is captured by the camera entering Bluewater bus station whilst operating the 96 from Woolwich. (Liam Farrer-Beddall)

Metroline took stock of twenty-three Gemini 3-bodied B5LHs for use on the 7. These arrived between May and July 2014, and were allocated Perivale. VWH2016 (LK14 FBN) represents the batch, and is seen passing through Marble Arch bound for East Acton. (Liam Farrer-Beddall)

Between October and December 2014, Metroline took stock of thirty-eight Gemini 3-bodied B5LHs. They were allocated to Potters Bar garage, and shared between routes 34 (Barnet–Edmonton) and 125 (Winchmore Hill–Colindale). VWH2042 (LK64 EHL) is seen in Barnet starting its return trip to Walthamstow. (Liam Farrer-Beddall)

Route 125 has the small PVR of the two routes taken up by Metroline in early 2015. VWH2060 (LK64 EJF) is seen setting out on its journey to Winchmore Hill, the infamous Southgate Underground station building being seen on the right of the photograph. (Liam Farrer-Beddall)

The final batch of original style Gemini 3s to be purchased by Metroline entered service from Willesden garage from where they were used on the 6 (Willesden–Holborn). VWH2119 (LK15 CXU) is photographed at Trafalgar Square heading towards Willesden. (Liam Farrer-Beddall)

A modest batch of eleven original style Gemini 3s were purchased by Tower Transit for use on the 212 between Chingford station and St James Street. The first of the batch, VH38101 (BF15 KFV), is seen departing Walthamstow Central for its journey to Chingford. (Liam Farrer-Beddall)

London United took stock of the last batch of original style Gemini 3-bodied B5LHs for route 285 (Heathrow Central–Kingston). VH40 (LJ15 JZT) represents the batch in this photograph, and is seen departing Cromwell Road bus station, Kingston. (Liam Farrer-Beddall)

March 2016 saw the fleets of London United and London Sovereign renumbered into a five-digit numbering sequence. VH44 (LJ15 LAA) took up the new identity of VH45144. It is captured by the camera heading towards Heathrow Central, having just passed the British Airways hangars at Heathrow, which can be viewed in the background. (Liam Farrer-Beddall)

As has already been mentioned in this book, two Gemini 3-bodied Volvo B5TLs were placed on loan with two London operators back in late 2013. In August 2015, the pair were acquired by Go-Ahead London and placed under the care of the Metrobus division. They took up rolling stock numbers WVL509 and WVL510 respectively. The latter vehicle, registered BF63 HDG, is seen passing through Croydon en route for Redhill on route 405. Sister vehicle BF63 HDE can be seen earlier in this book. (Liam Farrer-Beddall)

Go-Ahead London's Metrobus division took stock of the first of the restyled Gemini 3 models in 2015. WHV42 to WHV80 were allocated to Croydon garage, and put to use on the 119 (Bromley North–Purley Way) and the 202 (Blackheath–Crystal Palace). WHV48 (BP15 OLT) is seen in Croydon heading towards Purley Way. (Liam Farrer-Beddall)

The thirty-nine WHVs purchased by Go-Ahead London for the 119 and 202 services in south London arrived between August and October 2015. WHV69 (BF65 WJU) was one of the October deliveries. It is seen parked on layover at Crystal Palace bus station before heading back to Blackheath on the 202, this route requiring fewer vehicles than the 119. (Liam Farrer-Beddall)

The next batch of WHVs comprised twenty-four vehicles, all allocated to Merton garage. They were used on the 155 between Elephant & Castle and St George's Hospital in Tooting. WHV85 (BD65 EVP) is seen passing through Tooting Broadway shortly before reaching its terminus at St George's Hospital, Tooting. (Liam Farrer-Beddall)

Go-Ahead London's Sutton garage received the smallest batch of Gemini 3-bodied B5LHs, arriving in December 2015. They were intended for operation on the 93 (North Cheam–Putney Bridge). WHV106 (BT65 JGO) is photographed in Sutton heading for West Croydon on the 154. (Liam Farrer-Beddall)

Putney High Street was the most polluted road in London in the mid-2010s. To help combat this, Go-Ahead London purchased forty-one Gemini 3s, which operated alongside a fleet of Enviro 400 MMCs, displacing the older buses operating from Putney garage at the time. Routes 14, 22, 74 and 430 benefited from these vehicles which arrived over the winter of 2016. WHV117 (BV66 VHU) is seen passing through Marble Arch on its way to Baker Street station. David Beddall

Another of Putney's allocation is captured by the camera running through central London. Hyde Park Corner finds WHV142 (BT66 MSU) travelling out of service. (Liam Farrer-Beddall)

A batch of fifteen WHVs slotted in between the two batches allocated to Putney, being allocated to Morden Wharf for route 1 (Holborn–Canada Water). Representing this batch is WHV145 (BV66 VJO), and is seen departing Canada Water bus station for its journey to central London. (Liam Farrer-Beddall)

The final twenty-nine WHVs were delivered to Go-Ahead London over the course of October and November 2017. They were allocated to Morden Wharf garage where they were mostly used on the 188 (North Greenwich–Russell Square). WHV192 (LF67 EYC) is seen passing through Greenwich, flagged by the Cutty Sark. (Liam Farrer-Beddall)

Metroline took no less than 267 new style Gemini 3-bodied B5LHs between October 2015 and February 2018. They were used to replace the majority of Plaxton Presidents in the fleet. The first twenty-three of the type were allocated to Willesden garage for use on the 295 (Ladbrooke Grove Sainsbury's–Clapham Junction). VWH2129 (LK65 EBJ) is photographed at Shepherd's Bush Green. (Liam Farrer-Beddall)

VWH2185 (LK16 HZC) is the penultimate member of a batch of Gemini 3s allocated to Uxbridge for route 114. It is seen at journey's end at Ruislip station before heading back to Mill Hill Broadway via Harrow. (Liam Farrer-Beddall)

2018 saw the branding of a number of routes operating into the Hayes and Harlington area of West London. One route was the 140. VWH2190 (LK16 HZU) shows off the route branding applied to a number of the fleet used on the service. it is seen approaching the access tunnel to Heathrow's Central area. (Liam Farrer-Beddall)

Another Heathrow-bound route 140 bus is captured loading outside Hayes and Harlington station. The vehicle in question is VWH2211 (LK66 DWC). It shows off the roundel and the subtle hybrid logo applied to London's buses. (Liam Farrer-Beddall)

Fifty-seven VWHs (VWH2187–2243) were allocated to Harrow Weald to update the rolling stock on the 140 and 182. The batch arrived between June and October 2016. VWH2224 (LK16 HZT) is seen departing Brent Cross bound for Harrow Weald, Oxhey Lane. (Liam Farrer-Beddall)

Another member of the fifty-seven-strong batch allocated to Harrow Weald is seen approaching Harrow bus station on its journey from Heathrow. VWH2242 (LK66 EOM) is seen in this view shortly after being delivered to Metroline. (Liam Farrer-Beddall)

Willesden and Uxbridge took stock of the final 127 Gemini 3-bodied B5LHs. Those at Willesden were put to use on the 6 and 98. VWH2307 (LK17 DFC) is seen heading to its home garage, photographed at Marble Arch. (Liam Farrer-Beddall)

Those delivered to Willesden garage were also used to convert route 260 to the type, displacing Plaxton Presidents on the route. VWH2368 (LK67 CYC) is seen here passing Golders Green bus station carrying an all-over advertisement for the BBC Sounds app. (Liam Farrer-Beddall)

The 52 was another of Willesden's double-deck routes to benefit from the VWH class. VWH2425 (LK67 EZO) is seen loading at Notting Hill Gate bound for Victoria. (Liam Farrer-Beddall)

Twenty-five new style Gemini 3s were taken into stock by Tower Transit in March 2016. They were allocated to Atlas Road, and were put to use on the 328 (Chelsea, World's End–Golders Green). VH38128 (BU16 UXT) is seen at the latter location. (Liam Farrer-Beddall)

Between them the London United and London Sovereign fleets took stock of 132 new style Gemini 3-bodied B5LHs for operations on various routes. One of these routes was the 94 (Piccadilly Circus–Acton Green), which was operated from Shepherd's Bush garage. VH45155 (LJ16 FZM) is seen pulling away from the Selfridges stop on Oxford Street. (Liam Farrer-Beddall)

Metroline lost the contract for the 18 (Euston–Sudbury), with RATP London gaining the contract. Thirty-six Gemini 3-bodied B5LHs were taken into stock for use on the route, being allocated to Park Royal garage, the former Tower Transit Atlas Road site. VH45221 (BF67 GKF) is seen at Euston station before setting off for Sudbury. (Liam Farrer-Beddall)

June 2018 saw London United take over route 105 (Greenford station–Heathrow Airport) from Metroline. For the route, sixteen B5LHs were purchased. VH45273 (LF18 AXS) represents the batch, seen approaching Heathrow Central area. It is followed by a similar vehicle operated by Metroline. (Liam Farrer-Beddall)

The summer of 2018 saw twelve Gemini 3s delivered to London Sovereign for use on the H12 (Stanmore station–South Harrow). One of the batch, VH45307 (LF68 PYS), is captured by the camera at South Harrow station shortly after its arrival in London. (Liam Farrer-Beddall)

Arriva London won the contract for the 259 (Kings Cross–Edmonton Green) from Go-Ahead London in 2016. The service commenced in the spring of 2017, the fleet of twenty-five HV-class Volvo B5LHs arriving in plenty of time. HV203 (LK66 HCH) is seen about to enter Edmonton Green bus station. (Liam Farrer-Beddall)

January and February 2017 saw the arrival of twenty-three additional HVs, this time for Clapton garage. They were put to use on the 242 (Homerton Hospital–Tottenham Court Road), replacing the 09-plate Gemini 2s. HV235 (LK66 GBX) is seen passing through Dalston Junction heading north to Homerton. (Liam Farrer-Beddall)

Between August and November 2017 fifty-six Gemini 3-bodied Volvo B5LHs were taken into stock by Arriva London at Tottenham. They were put to use on the 243 and 341. HV352 (LF67 EUX) is photographed entering Aldwych, having just travelled across Waterloo Bridge. (Liam Farrer-Beddall)

Another thirty-three Gemini 3s arrived at Norwood to convert routes 2 (Norwood–Marylebone) and 468 (South Croydon–Elephant & Castle) to the type, the latter route being another gain from Go-Ahead London. HV381 (LC67 AHF) is seen operating the 468, crossing the tram tracks in Croydon. (Liam Farrer-Beddall)

Another member of the thirty-three-strong fleet of HVs delivered to Norwood at the beginning of 2018 was HV407 (LC67 AKO). It is seen heading towards its central London terminus of Marylebone, passing through Marble Arch. (Liam Farrer-Beddall)

The difference between the Gemini 2 and Gemini 3 models can be clearly seen in this photograph. The Tenyson Way stops at Waterloo finds Go-Ahead London's Gemini 3-bodied B5LH WHV189 (LF67 EXZ) and London Sovereign's Gemini 2-bodied B5LH VH45112 (BT13 YWK). (Liam Farrer-Beddall)

The Gemini 2's main competitor was the ADL Enviro 400. As can be seen in the photograph above, there was a distinct difference between the two models. Arriva London's Gemini 2 DW441 (LJ11 ACF) and Go-Ahead London's Enviro 400 E129 (SN60 BZA) are captured by the camera at Bexleyheath town centre. (Liam Farrer-Beddall)

Ensignbus, Purfleet, purchased a large number of Wright Eclipse Geminis from the Go-Ahead London Group in 2016 and 2017, mostly for resale. Former WVL150 (LX53 BJO) was used by Ensign in their rail replacement fleet. Numbered 908 by the new owner, it is seen approaching Romford station on rail replacement work. (Liam Farrer-Beddall)

37986 (BJ11 ECY) was a Wright Eclipse Gemini 2-bodied Volvo B9TL new to First Berkshire in August 2011. It was used by the company on its Green Line 702 service between London Victoria and Bracknell/Windsor. It is seen wearing Green Line livery shortly before completing its journey to Victoria. (Liam Farrer-Beddall)

37998 (BF63 HDX) was another Gemini 2-bodied B9TL double-decker purchased by First Berkshire for the 702 Green Line service, arriving in November 2013. It is seen passing the gardens of Buckingham Palace on its way to Legoland, Windsor. (Liam Farrer-Beddall)